50 Dinner Party Perfection Recipes

By: Kelly Johnson

Table of Contents

- Beef Wellington
- Lobster Tail with Garlic Butter
- Grilled Lemon Herb Chicken Skewers
- Eggplant Parmesan
- Shrimp Scampi
- Stuffed Mushrooms
- Roasted Chicken with Lemon and Rosemary
- Classic Beef Bourguignon
- Baked Ziti with Sausage
- Pan-Seared Scallops with Truffle Oil
- Caesar Salad with Homemade Dressing
- Mushroom Risotto
- Braised Short Ribs
- Sweet Potato Gratin
- Tuna Tartare
- Grilled Vegetable Platter
- Pork Tenderloin with Apple Chutney

- Ratatouille
- Grilled Ribeye Steaks with Chimichurri
- Lobster Mac and Cheese
- Chicken Cacciatore
- Beef and Broccoli Stir Fry
- Moroccan Lamb Tagine
- Fettuccine Alfredo
- Roasted Brussels Sprouts with Balsamic Glaze
- Crab Cakes with Remoulade Sauce
- Quinoa and Roasted Vegetable Salad
- Duck Breast with Cherry Sauce
- Seared Tuna with Wasabi Aioli
- Butternut Squash Soup
- Grilled Flatbreads with Toppings
- Filet Mignon with Garlic Butter
- Chicken Marsala
- Spaghetti Aglio e Olio
- Grilled Shrimp Tacos with Mango Salsa
- Egg Salad on Croissants

- Truffle Mac and Cheese
- Stuffed Bell Peppers
- Pulled Pork Sliders
- Lobster Bisque
- Beef Tacos with Cilantro Lime Crema
- Spinach and Ricotta Stuffed Pasta Shells
- Chicken Piccata
- Thai Green Curry with Vegetables
- Grilled Salmon with Avocado Salsa
- Baked Brie with Fig Jam
- Prosciutto-Wrapped Asparagus
- Braised Lamb Shanks
- Vegetable Paella
- Spicy Tuna Roll Sushi

Beef Wellington

Ingredients:

- 1.5 lbs beef tenderloin
- 2 tbsp olive oil
- 2 tbsp Dijon mustard
- 1 lb mushrooms, finely chopped
- 2 tbsp butter
- 2 cloves garlic, minced
- 1/2 cup dry white wine
- 1/2 cup heavy cream
- 8 oz prosciutto
- 1 sheet puff pastry
- 1 egg, beaten
- Salt and pepper to taste

Instructions:

1. Sear the beef tenderloin in olive oil over medium-high heat until browned on all sides. Brush with Dijon mustard and let cool.

2. In a skillet, sauté garlic and mushrooms in butter until the mushrooms release their moisture and the mixture is dry. Add wine, cook until absorbed, and stir in cream.

3. Lay out the prosciutto, spread the mushroom mixture on top, and roll the beef inside. Wrap with puff pastry and brush with egg wash.

4. Bake at 400°F (200°C) for 30-35 minutes, or until golden brown. Let rest before slicing.

Lobster Tail with Garlic Butter

Ingredients:

- 4 lobster tails
- 4 tbsp unsalted butter, melted
- 3 cloves garlic, minced
- 1 tbsp lemon juice
- Salt and pepper to taste
- Fresh parsley, chopped

Instructions:

1. Preheat the oven to 425°F (220°C).
2. Using kitchen shears, cut the top shell of the lobster tails, exposing the meat. Place on a baking sheet.
3. Mix melted butter, garlic, lemon juice, salt, and pepper. Pour over the lobster meat.
4. Bake for 12-15 minutes, or until the meat is opaque and cooked through. Garnish with fresh parsley.

Grilled Lemon Herb Chicken Skewers

Ingredients:

- 2 lbs boneless chicken breast, cut into cubes
- 1/4 cup olive oil
- 2 tbsp lemon juice
- 2 cloves garlic, minced
- 1 tbsp fresh thyme, chopped
- 1 tbsp fresh rosemary, chopped
- Salt and pepper to taste
- Wooden skewers (soaked in water)

Instructions:

1. In a bowl, mix olive oil, lemon juice, garlic, thyme, rosemary, salt, and pepper. Marinate the chicken for at least 30 minutes.
2. Thread the chicken onto the skewers.
3. Grill over medium-high heat for 6-8 minutes per side, or until fully cooked. Serve with lemon wedges.

Eggplant Parmesan

Ingredients:

- 2 large eggplants, sliced into 1/2-inch rounds
- 2 cups marinara sauce
- 1 1/2 cups mozzarella cheese, shredded
- 1/2 cup grated Parmesan cheese
- 1 cup breadcrumbs
- 2 eggs, beaten
- 1/4 cup flour
- Olive oil for frying
- Salt and pepper to taste

Instructions:

1. Season eggplant slices with salt and let them sit for 30 minutes. Pat dry.
2. Dip each slice in flour, then egg, and coat with breadcrumbs.
3. Fry in olive oil until golden on both sides, then drain on paper towels.
4. Preheat oven to 375°F (190°C). Layer fried eggplant, marinara sauce, mozzarella, and Parmesan in a baking dish. Repeat layers.
5. Bake for 25-30 minutes until bubbly and golden.

Shrimp Scampi

Ingredients:

- 1 lb large shrimp, peeled and deveined
- 4 tbsp butter
- 4 cloves garlic, minced
- 1/4 cup white wine
- 2 tbsp lemon juice
- 1/2 tsp red pepper flakes
- 1/4 cup fresh parsley, chopped
- Salt and pepper to taste
- 8 oz spaghetti

Instructions:

1. Cook the spaghetti according to package directions.
2. In a large skillet, melt butter over medium heat. Add garlic and red pepper flakes and sauté until fragrant.
3. Add shrimp, white wine, lemon juice, salt, and pepper. Cook until shrimp turn pink, about 3-4 minutes.
4. Toss the cooked pasta with the shrimp mixture, garnish with parsley, and serve.

Stuffed Mushrooms

Ingredients:

- 16 large mushrooms, stems removed
- 4 oz cream cheese, softened
- 1/4 cup grated Parmesan cheese
- 2 cloves garlic, minced
- 1/4 cup breadcrumbs
- 1/4 cup fresh parsley, chopped
- Salt and pepper to taste
- Olive oil for drizzling

Instructions:

1. Preheat the oven to 375°F (190°C).
2. Mix cream cheese, Parmesan, garlic, breadcrumbs, parsley, salt, and pepper in a bowl.
3. Stuff each mushroom cap with the cream cheese mixture.
4. Arrange on a baking sheet, drizzle with olive oil, and bake for 20 minutes, or until golden brown.

Roasted Chicken with Lemon and Rosemary

Ingredients:

- 1 whole chicken (about 4 lbs)
- 2 lemons, quartered
- 3 sprigs fresh rosemary
- 1 head garlic, halved
- 1/4 cup olive oil
- Salt and pepper to taste

Instructions:

1. Preheat oven to 425°F (220°C).
2. Stuff the chicken with lemon, rosemary, and garlic. Rub the outside with olive oil, salt, and pepper.
3. Roast for 1 hour and 15 minutes, or until the internal temperature reaches 165°F (75°C). Let rest before carving.

Classic Beef Bourguignon

Ingredients:

- 3 lbs beef chuck, cut into 1-inch cubes
- 2 tbsp olive oil
- 1 onion, chopped
- 3 carrots, chopped
- 3 cloves garlic, minced
- 1 cup red wine
- 2 cups beef broth
- 1 bouquet garni (thyme, bay leaves, parsley)
- 1 tbsp tomato paste
- 2 cups pearl onions
- 2 cups mushrooms, sliced
- Salt and pepper to taste

Instructions:

1. Brown beef in olive oil in batches. Remove and set aside.
2. In the same pot, sauté onions, carrots, and garlic until softened.
3. Stir in tomato paste, wine, broth, and bouquet garni. Return beef to the pot and bring to a boil.
4. Lower heat, cover, and simmer for 2-3 hours, until beef is tender.

5. Sauté pearl onions and mushrooms in butter and add to the stew. Cook for another 15-20 minutes. Season with salt and pepper.

Baked Ziti with Sausage

Ingredients:

- 1 lb ziti pasta
- 1 lb Italian sausage, casing removed
- 4 cups marinara sauce
- 2 cups ricotta cheese
- 2 cups mozzarella cheese, shredded
- 1/2 cup Parmesan cheese, grated
- 1 tbsp fresh basil, chopped
- Salt and pepper to taste

Instructions:

1. Preheat oven to 375°F (190°C).
2. Cook pasta according to package directions. Drain and set aside.
3. Brown sausage in a skillet, breaking it apart as it cooks.
4. Mix pasta, sausage, marinara sauce, and ricotta in a bowl. Transfer to a baking dish and top with mozzarella and Parmesan.
5. Bake for 20 minutes, or until bubbly and golden. Garnish with basil.

Pan-Seared Scallops with Truffle Oil

Ingredients:

- 1 lb large sea scallops
- 2 tbsp olive oil
- 1 tbsp butter
- 1 tbsp truffle oil
- Salt and pepper to taste
- Fresh parsley, chopped

Instructions:

1. Pat scallops dry and season with salt and pepper.
2. Heat olive oil and butter in a pan over high heat. Once hot, add scallops and sear for 2-3 minutes per side.
3. Drizzle with truffle oil and garnish with fresh parsley. Serve immediately.

Caesar Salad with Homemade Dressing

Ingredients:

- 1 large head romaine lettuce, chopped
- 1/2 cup grated Parmesan cheese
- 1 cup croutons

For the dressing:

- 1/4 cup mayonnaise
- 2 tbsp Dijon mustard
- 2 tbsp lemon juice
- 2 cloves garlic, minced
- 1 tbsp anchovy paste
- 1/2 tsp Worcestershire sauce
- Salt and pepper to taste
- 1/4 cup olive oil

Instructions:

1. For the dressing, whisk together mayonnaise, mustard, lemon juice, garlic, anchovy paste, Worcestershire sauce, salt, and pepper. Gradually whisk in olive oil until smooth.
2. Toss lettuce with dressing and top with Parmesan and croutons.

Mushroom Risotto

Ingredients:

- 2 tbsp olive oil
- 1 onion, chopped
- 2 cups Arborio rice
- 1/2 cup white wine
- 4 cups chicken or vegetable broth, kept warm
- 2 cups mushrooms, sliced
- 1/2 cup Parmesan cheese, grated
- 2 tbsp butter
- Salt and pepper to taste

Instructions:

1. Heat olive oil in a large pan over medium heat. Sauté onions until soft, about 5 minutes.
2. Stir in rice and cook for 2 minutes. Add wine and cook until absorbed.
3. Gradually add warm broth, one ladle at a time, stirring constantly until absorbed before adding more. Continue until the rice is tender and creamy, about 18-20 minutes.
4. Stir in mushrooms, Parmesan, butter, salt, and pepper. Serve immediately.

Braised Short Ribs

Ingredients:

- 4 lbs bone-in beef short ribs
- 2 tbsp olive oil
- 1 onion, chopped
- 2 carrots, chopped
- 2 celery stalks, chopped
- 4 cloves garlic, minced
- 1 cup red wine
- 2 cups beef broth
- 1 tbsp tomato paste
- 1 sprig rosemary
- 2 sprigs thyme
- Salt and pepper to taste

Instructions:

1. Preheat oven to 350°F (175°C).
2. Season short ribs with salt and pepper. Brown in olive oil over medium-high heat in a large pot. Remove and set aside.
3. Add onion, carrots, celery, and garlic to the pot and sauté until softened. Stir in tomato paste.

4. Pour in wine, scraping the bottom of the pot. Add broth, rosemary, thyme, and short ribs.

5. Cover and braise in the oven for 2.5-3 hours, until tender. Serve with sauce.

Sweet Potato Gratin

Ingredients:

- 4 large sweet potatoes, peeled and thinly sliced
- 2 cups heavy cream
- 1/2 cup milk
- 2 cloves garlic, minced
- 1/2 tsp ground nutmeg
- 1 cup grated Gruyère cheese
- 1 tbsp butter, for greasing
- Salt and pepper to taste

Instructions:

1. Preheat oven to 375°F (190°C). Grease a baking dish with butter.
2. In a saucepan, heat cream, milk, garlic, nutmeg, salt, and pepper until warm.
3. Layer sweet potato slices in the baking dish, pouring the cream mixture over each layer. Top with Gruyère cheese.
4. Cover with foil and bake for 40 minutes. Uncover and bake for an additional 20 minutes, or until golden and tender.

Tuna Tartare

Ingredients:

- 1 lb fresh tuna, sushi-grade, diced
- 1/4 cup soy sauce
- 1 tbsp sesame oil
- 1 tsp fresh lime juice
- 1 tbsp fresh cilantro, chopped
- 1 tbsp green onions, chopped
- 1 tsp toasted sesame seeds
- 1/4 avocado, diced
- 1 small cucumber, thinly sliced

Instructions:

1. In a bowl, combine tuna, soy sauce, sesame oil, lime juice, cilantro, green onions, and sesame seeds.
2. Gently fold in avocado and cucumber.
3. Serve immediately with crackers or on a bed of greens.

Grilled Vegetable Platter

Ingredients:

- 1 zucchini, sliced
- 1 yellow squash, sliced
- 1 bell pepper, cut into strips
- 1 red onion, sliced
- 8 oz mushrooms, halved
- 2 tbsp olive oil
- 1 tbsp balsamic vinegar
- Salt and pepper to taste

Instructions:

1. Preheat grill to medium-high heat.
2. Toss vegetables in olive oil, balsamic vinegar, salt, and pepper.
3. Grill vegetables for 3-4 minutes per side, or until tender and slightly charred.
4. Arrange on a platter and serve warm.

Pork Tenderloin with Apple Chutney

Ingredients:

- 1 pork tenderloin (about 1 lb)
- 2 tbsp olive oil
- Salt and pepper to taste

For the apple chutney:

- 2 apples, peeled and diced
- 1/2 onion, chopped
- 1/4 cup apple cider vinegar
- 1/4 cup brown sugar
- 1/4 tsp ground cinnamon
- 1/4 tsp ground ginger
- Salt to taste

Instructions:

1. Preheat oven to 400°F (200°C).
2. Season the pork tenderloin with salt and pepper. Sear in olive oil over medium-high heat until browned on all sides. Transfer to the oven and roast for 20-25 minutes, or until the internal temperature reaches 145°F (63°C).
3. For the chutney, combine all ingredients in a saucepan. Simmer over low heat for 20-25 minutes, stirring occasionally, until thickened.

4. Serve the pork tenderloin with apple chutney on top.

Ratatouille

Ingredients:

- 1 eggplant, diced
- 2 zucchini, diced
- 1 bell pepper, chopped
- 1 onion, chopped
- 2 tomatoes, chopped
- 2 cloves garlic, minced
- 1/4 cup olive oil
- 1 tbsp fresh basil, chopped
- Salt and pepper to taste

Instructions:

1. Heat olive oil in a large skillet over medium heat. Add onion and garlic, sautéing until softened.
2. Add eggplant, zucchini, bell pepper, and tomatoes. Season with salt and pepper.
3. Simmer for 20-25 minutes, stirring occasionally. Garnish with fresh basil before serving.

Grilled Ribeye Steaks with Chimichurri

Ingredients:

- 2 ribeye steaks
- Salt and pepper to taste

For the chimichurri:

- 1 cup fresh parsley, chopped
- 3 cloves garlic, minced
- 1/4 cup red wine vinegar
- 1/2 cup olive oil
- 1/2 tsp red pepper flakes
- Salt and pepper to taste

Instructions:

1. Preheat grill to high heat.
2. Season steaks with salt and pepper. Grill for 4-6 minutes per side, or until desired doneness.
3. For the chimichurri, combine parsley, garlic, vinegar, olive oil, red pepper flakes, salt, and pepper in a bowl.
4. Serve steaks topped with chimichurri sauce.

Lobster Mac and Cheese

Ingredients:

- 2 lobster tails, cooked and chopped
- 1 lb elbow macaroni
- 2 cups shredded sharp cheddar cheese
- 1/2 cup grated Parmesan cheese
- 2 tbsp butter
- 2 tbsp flour
- 2 cups milk
- 1/2 tsp mustard powder
- Salt and pepper to taste
- 1/4 cup breadcrumbs

Instructions:

1. Cook macaroni according to package directions.

2. In a saucepan, melt butter and whisk in flour. Gradually add milk, whisking until smooth. Stir in cheddar, Parmesan, mustard powder, salt, and pepper until creamy.

3. Mix in cooked macaroni and lobster. Transfer to a baking dish, top with breadcrumbs, and bake at 350°F (175°C) for 20 minutes, until golden and bubbly.

Chicken Cacciatore

Ingredients:

- 4 chicken thighs, bone-in, skin-on
- 2 tbsp olive oil
- 1 onion, chopped
- 2 bell peppers, chopped
- 4 cloves garlic, minced
- 1 can (14.5 oz) diced tomatoes
- 1 cup dry white wine
- 1 tsp dried oregano
- 1/2 tsp red pepper flakes
- Salt and pepper to taste
- Fresh basil, chopped

Instructions:

1. Heat olive oil in a large pan over medium-high heat. Brown chicken thighs on both sides. Remove and set aside.
2. In the same pan, sauté onion, bell peppers, and garlic until softened.
3. Add diced tomatoes, white wine, oregano, red pepper flakes, salt, and pepper. Return chicken to the pan, skin side up.
4. Cover and simmer for 30-40 minutes, or until chicken is cooked through. Garnish with fresh basil before serving.

Chicken Cacciatore

Ingredients:

- 4 chicken thighs (bone-in, skin-on)
- 2 tbsp olive oil
- 1 onion, chopped
- 2 cloves garlic, minced
- 1 bell pepper, chopped
- 1 can (14.5 oz) diced tomatoes
- 1/2 cup dry white wine
- 1/2 cup chicken broth
- 1/4 cup Kalamata olives, pitted and sliced
- 2 tbsp capers
- 1 tbsp fresh oregano, chopped
- Salt and pepper to taste

Instructions:

1. Heat olive oil in a large pan over medium heat. Season chicken thighs with salt and pepper, then brown on both sides, about 5-6 minutes per side. Remove and set aside.

2. In the same pan, add onion, garlic, and bell pepper. Sauté until softened, about 5 minutes.

3. Add diced tomatoes, white wine, chicken broth, olives, capers, and oregano. Stir to combine.

4. Return chicken to the pan, cover, and simmer for 30-40 minutes, until the chicken is cooked through.

5. Serve with pasta or crusty bread.

Beef and Broccoli Stir Fry

Ingredients:

- 1 lb beef sirloin, thinly sliced
- 2 cups broccoli florets
- 2 tbsp vegetable oil
- 3 cloves garlic, minced
- 1/4 cup soy sauce
- 1 tbsp oyster sauce
- 1 tbsp hoisin sauce
- 1 tbsp cornstarch
- 1/2 cup beef broth
- 1 tsp sesame oil
- 1 tsp fresh ginger, grated

Instructions:

1. In a bowl, mix soy sauce, oyster sauce, hoisin sauce, cornstarch, and beef broth. Set aside.

2. Heat vegetable oil in a large skillet or wok over medium-high heat. Add beef and cook until browned. Remove and set aside.

3. In the same pan, sauté garlic and ginger until fragrant, about 1 minute.

4. Add broccoli and stir fry for 2-3 minutes. Return beef to the pan and pour in the sauce mixture. Cook for an additional 3-4 minutes, until thickened.

5. Drizzle with sesame oil before serving.

Moroccan Lamb Tagine

Ingredients:

- 2 lbs lamb shoulder, cut into cubes
- 2 tbsp olive oil
- 1 onion, chopped
- 3 cloves garlic, minced
- 1 tbsp ground cumin
- 1 tsp ground cinnamon
- 1/2 tsp ground turmeric
- 1/4 tsp ground ginger
- 1/4 tsp ground coriander
- 1 can (14.5 oz) diced tomatoes
- 1 cup beef broth
- 1/2 cup dried apricots, chopped
- 1/4 cup almonds, toasted
- Fresh cilantro for garnish
- Salt and pepper to taste

Instructions:

1. In a large pot or tagine, heat olive oil over medium heat. Brown lamb cubes on all sides. Remove and set aside.

2. Add onion and garlic to the pot and sauté until softened. Stir in spices and cook for 1-2 minutes.

3. Add diced tomatoes, beef broth, and apricots. Return lamb to the pot. Bring to a simmer, cover, and cook for 1.5-2 hours, until the lamb is tender.

4. Garnish with toasted almonds and fresh cilantro. Serve with couscous or flatbread.

Fettuccine Alfredo

Ingredients:

- 1 lb fettuccine pasta
- 2 tbsp butter
- 2 cups heavy cream
- 1 cup grated Parmesan cheese
- 1/2 tsp garlic powder
- Salt and pepper to taste
- Fresh parsley for garnish

Instructions:

1. Cook fettuccine according to package directions. Drain, reserving 1 cup of pasta water.

2. In a large pan, melt butter over medium heat. Add heavy cream and bring to a simmer. Cook for 5-7 minutes, until thickened.

3. Stir in Parmesan, garlic powder, salt, and pepper. Toss the cooked pasta into the sauce, adding reserved pasta water as needed to reach desired consistency.

4. Garnish with fresh parsley and serve.

Roasted Brussels Sprouts with Balsamic Glaze

Ingredients:

- 1 lb Brussels sprouts, trimmed and halved
- 2 tbsp olive oil
- Salt and pepper to taste
- 2 tbsp balsamic vinegar
- 1 tbsp honey

Instructions:

1. Preheat oven to 400°F (200°C).
2. Toss Brussels sprouts with olive oil, salt, and pepper. Spread on a baking sheet in a single layer.
3. Roast for 25-30 minutes, shaking the pan halfway through.
4. In a small saucepan, heat balsamic vinegar and honey over medium heat. Simmer for 5-7 minutes until thickened.
5. Drizzle balsamic glaze over roasted Brussels sprouts before serving.

Crab Cakes with Remoulade Sauce

Ingredients:

- 1 lb crab meat
- 1/2 cup breadcrumbs
- 1/4 cup mayonnaise
- 1 egg, beaten
- 1 tbsp Dijon mustard
- 2 tbsp fresh parsley, chopped
- 1 tsp Old Bay seasoning
- 2 tbsp olive oil

For the remoulade sauce:

- 1/2 cup mayonnaise
- 1 tbsp Dijon mustard
- 1 tbsp lemon juice
- 1 tsp hot sauce
- 1 tsp paprika
- Salt to taste

Instructions:

1. In a bowl, combine crab meat, breadcrumbs, mayonnaise, egg, Dijon mustard, parsley, and Old Bay seasoning. Form into patties.

2. Heat olive oil in a skillet over medium heat. Cook crab cakes for 3-4 minutes per side, until golden brown.

3. For the remoulade sauce, mix all ingredients in a small bowl. Serve crab cakes with sauce on the side.

Quinoa and Roasted Vegetable Salad

Ingredients:

- 1 cup quinoa
- 2 cups water
- 1 zucchini, chopped
- 1 bell pepper, chopped
- 1 red onion, chopped
- 1 tbsp olive oil
- Salt and pepper to taste
- 1/4 cup feta cheese, crumbled
- Fresh parsley for garnish

For the dressing:

- 2 tbsp olive oil
- 1 tbsp lemon juice
- 1 tsp Dijon mustard
- Salt and pepper to taste

Instructions:

1. Preheat oven to 400°F (200°C).

2. Toss zucchini, bell pepper, and onion with olive oil, salt, and pepper. Roast for 20-25 minutes, until tender.

3. Meanwhile, cook quinoa in water according to package instructions.

4. For the dressing, whisk together olive oil, lemon juice, Dijon mustard, salt, and pepper.

5. Toss quinoa with roasted vegetables, feta, and dressing. Garnish with fresh parsley before serving.

Duck Breast with Cherry Sauce

Ingredients:

- 2 duck breasts
- Salt and pepper to taste
- 1/2 cup red wine
- 1/2 cup chicken broth
- 1/2 cup fresh or frozen cherries, pitted
- 1 tbsp balsamic vinegar
- 1 tbsp honey

Instructions:

1. Preheat oven to 400°F (200°C).
2. Score the skin of the duck breasts. Season with salt and pepper.
3. Sear duck breasts, skin side down, in a hot pan with oil for 6-8 minutes. Flip and cook for an additional 3-4 minutes. Transfer to the oven and roast for 5-7 minutes for medium-rare.
4. In the same pan, add wine, chicken broth, cherries, balsamic vinegar, and honey. Simmer until sauce thickens, about 10 minutes.
5. Serve duck with the cherry sauce.

Seared Tuna with Wasabi Aioli

Ingredients:

- 2 tuna steaks
- 1 tbsp sesame oil
- Salt and pepper to taste

For the wasabi aioli:

- 1/4 cup mayonnaise
- 1 tsp wasabi paste
- 1 tsp lemon juice
- Salt to taste

Instructions:

1. Heat sesame oil in a pan over high heat. Season tuna steaks with salt and pepper. Sear each side for 1-2 minutes for rare.
2. For the aioli, mix mayonnaise, wasabi paste, lemon juice, and salt in a bowl.
3. Serve tuna steaks with wasabi aioli.

Butternut Squash Soup

Ingredients:

- 1 butternut squash, peeled and diced
- 1 onion, chopped
- 2 carrots, chopped
- 2 cloves garlic, minced
- 4 cups vegetable broth
- 1/2 tsp ground nutmeg
- Salt and pepper to taste
- 1/2 cup heavy cream (optional)

Instructions:

1. In a large pot, sauté onion, carrots, and garlic in olive oil until softened.
2. Add butternut squash, vegetable broth, nutmeg, salt, and pepper. Bring to a simmer and cook until squash is tender, about 20 minutes.
3. Puree the soup with an immersion blender or in batches until smooth.
4. Stir in heavy cream, if desired, and adjust seasoning before serving.

Grilled Flatbreads with Toppings

Ingredients:

- 2 cups all-purpose flour
- 1 tsp active dry yeast
- 1/2 tsp sugar
- 3/4 cup warm water
- 2 tbsp olive oil
- Salt to taste
- Toppings of your choice: tomatoes, mozzarella, arugula, olives, onions, feta, etc.

Instructions:

1. In a small bowl, dissolve sugar in warm water and sprinkle yeast over the top. Let sit for 5-10 minutes until frothy.
2. In a large bowl, combine flour and salt. Add the yeast mixture and olive oil. Mix until a dough forms.
3. Knead the dough for 5-7 minutes until smooth. Cover and let it rise for 1-2 hours, or until doubled in size.
4. Preheat the grill to medium-high heat.
5. Punch down the dough and divide it into 4 portions. Roll each portion into a flatbread shape.
6. Place flatbreads on the grill and cook for 2-3 minutes per side, until golden and crisp.
7. Remove from the grill and add your desired toppings. Serve warm.

Filet Mignon with Garlic Butter

Ingredients:

- 2 filet mignon steaks (6-8 oz each)
- Salt and pepper to taste
- 2 tbsp olive oil
- 4 tbsp unsalted butter
- 4 cloves garlic, minced
- 2 sprigs fresh rosemary or thyme (optional)

Instructions:

1. Season the filet mignon steaks with salt and pepper on both sides.
2. Heat olive oil in a large skillet over medium-high heat. Add the steaks and cook for 4-5 minutes per side for medium-rare, or longer to your desired doneness.
3. While the steaks cook, melt butter in a separate small pan over medium heat. Add garlic and herbs, sautéing until fragrant, about 1-2 minutes.
4. Once the steaks are done, remove them from the skillet and let rest for 5 minutes.
5. Drizzle the garlic butter over the steaks before serving.

Chicken Marsala

Ingredients:

- 4 boneless, skinless chicken breasts
- Salt and pepper to taste
- 1/2 cup all-purpose flour
- 2 tbsp olive oil
- 1 cup mushrooms, sliced
- 1/2 cup Marsala wine
- 1/2 cup chicken broth
- 2 tbsp unsalted butter
- Fresh parsley for garnish

Instructions:

1. Season chicken breasts with salt and pepper, then dredge them in flour, shaking off the excess.
2. Heat olive oil in a large pan over medium heat. Add the chicken and cook for 5-6 minutes per side, until golden and cooked through. Remove chicken from the pan and set aside.
3. In the same pan, add mushrooms and sauté for 3-4 minutes until softened.
4. Add Marsala wine and chicken broth, scraping up any brown bits from the pan. Bring to a simmer and cook for 5 minutes.
5. Stir in butter until melted and the sauce thickens slightly.

6. Return the chicken to the pan and coat with the sauce. Simmer for 2-3 minutes.

7. Garnish with fresh parsley before serving.

Spaghetti Aglio e Olio

Ingredients:

- 12 oz spaghetti
- 1/4 cup olive oil
- 6 cloves garlic, thinly sliced
- 1/2 tsp red pepper flakes
- Salt to taste
- Fresh parsley, chopped
- Grated Parmesan cheese (optional)

Instructions:

1. Cook spaghetti according to package instructions. Reserve 1 cup of pasta water before draining.
2. In a large pan, heat olive oil over medium heat. Add garlic and red pepper flakes, sautéing until fragrant but not browned, about 2 minutes.
3. Add the cooked spaghetti to the pan, tossing to coat in the oil and garlic. If needed, add reserved pasta water to loosen the sauce.
4. Season with salt and toss with fresh parsley.
5. Serve with grated Parmesan cheese, if desired.

Grilled Shrimp Tacos with Mango Salsa

Ingredients:

- 1 lb shrimp, peeled and deveined
- 1 tbsp olive oil
- 1 tsp chili powder
- 1/2 tsp garlic powder
- Salt and pepper to taste
- 8 small soft tortillas
- 1 mango, peeled and diced
- 1/4 red onion, finely chopped
- 1/4 cup cilantro, chopped
- 1 tbsp lime juice

Instructions:

1. Preheat the grill to medium-high heat.
2. Toss shrimp with olive oil, chili powder, garlic powder, salt, and pepper.
3. Grill shrimp for 2-3 minutes per side, until pink and cooked through.
4. In a bowl, combine mango, red onion, cilantro, and lime juice. Stir to combine.
5. Assemble the tacos by placing grilled shrimp on tortillas and topping with mango salsa. Serve immediately.

Egg Salad on Croissants

Ingredients:

- 6 hard-boiled eggs, chopped
- 1/4 cup mayonnaise
- 1 tbsp Dijon mustard
- 1 tsp lemon juice
- Salt and pepper to taste
- 4 croissants, split
- Lettuce leaves for garnish

Instructions:

1. In a bowl, combine chopped eggs, mayonnaise, Dijon mustard, lemon juice, salt, and pepper. Stir to combine.
2. Slice croissants in half and layer with lettuce leaves.
3. Spoon egg salad onto the croissants and serve immediately.

Truffle Mac and Cheese

Ingredients:

- 1 lb elbow macaroni
- 2 tbsp butter
- 2 tbsp all-purpose flour
- 2 cups milk
- 2 cups shredded sharp cheddar cheese
- 1/2 cup grated Parmesan cheese
- 2 tbsp truffle oil
- Salt and pepper to taste

Instructions:

1. Cook macaroni according to package instructions, drain, and set aside.
2. In a saucepan, melt butter over medium heat. Stir in flour and cook for 1-2 minutes.
3. Gradually whisk in milk and bring to a simmer, cooking for 5-7 minutes until thickened.
4. Stir in cheddar cheese, Parmesan, and truffle oil until melted and smooth. Season with salt and pepper.
5. Toss the cooked macaroni in the sauce and serve.

Stuffed Bell Peppers

Ingredients:

- 4 bell peppers, tops cut off and seeds removed
- 1 lb ground beef or turkey
- 1/2 cup cooked rice
- 1 can (14.5 oz) diced tomatoes
- 1/2 cup shredded cheddar cheese
- 1/4 cup fresh parsley, chopped
- 1 tsp Italian seasoning
- Salt and pepper to taste

Instructions:

1. Preheat oven to 375°F (190°C).
2. In a pan, cook ground beef or turkey until browned. Add rice, diced tomatoes, Italian seasoning, salt, and pepper. Stir to combine.
3. Stuff the bell peppers with the meat mixture and place them in a baking dish.
4. Cover with foil and bake for 25 minutes. Remove foil and sprinkle with cheddar cheese. Bake for an additional 5-10 minutes until the cheese is melted.
5. Garnish with fresh parsley and serve.

Pulled Pork Sliders

Ingredients:

- 2 lbs pork shoulder
- 1 tbsp paprika
- 1 tsp garlic powder
- 1 tsp onion powder
- 1/2 tsp cayenne pepper
- Salt and pepper to taste
- 1 cup barbecue sauce
- 12 slider buns
- Coleslaw (optional)

Instructions:

1. Preheat oven to 300°F (150°C).
2. Rub pork shoulder with paprika, garlic powder, onion powder, cayenne pepper, salt, and pepper.
3. Place pork in a roasting pan and cover tightly with foil. Roast for 4-5 hours, until tender.
4. Shred the pork with two forks, then mix with barbecue sauce.
5. Serve on slider buns with coleslaw, if desired.

Lobster Bisque

Ingredients:

- 2 lobster tails, cooked and chopped
- 4 tbsp butter
- 1 onion, chopped
- 2 cloves garlic, minced
- 1/4 cup brandy or white wine
- 2 cups seafood or chicken broth
- 1 cup heavy cream
- Salt and pepper to taste
- Fresh parsley for garnish

Instructions:

1. In a large pot, melt butter over medium heat. Add onion and garlic and cook until softened.
2. Deglaze the pot with brandy or wine, scraping up any bits from the bottom.
3. Add broth and bring to a simmer. Cook for 10-15 minutes.
4. Stir in heavy cream and chopped lobster. Simmer for another 5 minutes.
5. Blend the soup using an immersion blender until smooth. Season with salt and pepper.
6. Garnish with fresh parsley before serving.

Beef Tacos with Cilantro Lime Crema

Ingredients:

- 1 lb ground beef
- 1 packet taco seasoning
- 1/4 cup water
- 8 small taco shells
- 1 cup shredded lettuce
- 1/2 cup diced tomatoes
- 1/4 cup diced red onion
- 1/4 cup shredded cheese (optional)
- 1/4 cup sour cream
- 2 tbsp fresh cilantro, chopped
- 1 tbsp lime juice
- Salt and pepper to taste

Instructions:

1. In a skillet, cook ground beef over medium heat until browned. Drain excess fat.
2. Add taco seasoning and water to the beef, simmer for 5 minutes, stirring occasionally.
3. While the beef cooks, prepare the cilantro lime crema by mixing sour cream, chopped cilantro, lime juice, salt, and pepper in a bowl.

4. Warm the taco shells in the oven or microwave.

5. Assemble the tacos by spooning the seasoned beef into each shell, and top with lettuce, tomatoes, onion, cheese, and a drizzle of cilantro lime crema. Serve immediately.

Spinach and Ricotta Stuffed Pasta Shells

Ingredients:

- 12 large pasta shells
- 2 cups ricotta cheese
- 1 cup cooked spinach, squeezed dry
- 1/2 cup grated Parmesan cheese
- 1 egg
- 2 cups marinara sauce
- 1 cup shredded mozzarella cheese
- Salt and pepper to taste
- Fresh basil for garnish (optional)

Instructions:

1. Preheat oven to 375°F (190°C). Cook pasta shells according to package instructions, drain, and set aside.

2. In a bowl, combine ricotta cheese, cooked spinach, Parmesan cheese, egg, salt, and pepper.

3. Spoon the ricotta-spinach mixture into each pasta shell.

4. In a baking dish, spread a thin layer of marinara sauce. Arrange the stuffed shells in the dish and cover with the remaining marinara sauce.

5. Sprinkle shredded mozzarella cheese on top.

6. Cover the dish with foil and bake for 20-25 minutes. Remove the foil and bake for an additional 5-10 minutes, until the cheese is bubbly and golden.

7. Garnish with fresh basil and serve.

Chicken Piccata

Ingredients:

- 4 boneless, skinless chicken breasts
- Salt and pepper to taste
- 1/2 cup flour, for dredging
- 3 tbsp olive oil
- 1/4 cup fresh lemon juice
- 1/2 cup chicken broth
- 2 tbsp capers, drained
- 2 tbsp unsalted butter
- Fresh parsley for garnish

Instructions:

1. Season chicken breasts with salt and pepper, then dredge them in flour, shaking off the excess.

2. In a large skillet, heat olive oil over medium-high heat. Cook chicken breasts for 4-5 minutes per side, until golden and cooked through. Remove chicken from the skillet and set aside.

3. In the same skillet, add lemon juice, chicken broth, and capers. Bring to a simmer and cook for 5 minutes, reducing the sauce slightly.

4. Stir in butter until melted and the sauce thickens.

5. Return chicken to the skillet and coat in the sauce. Simmer for another 2 minutes.

6. Garnish with fresh parsley and serve.

Thai Green Curry with Vegetables

Ingredients:

- 1 tbsp vegetable oil
- 1 onion, sliced
- 1 red bell pepper, sliced
- 1 zucchini, sliced
- 1/2 cup snap peas
- 1 can (14 oz) coconut milk
- 2 tbsp green curry paste
- 1 tbsp soy sauce
- 1 tbsp brown sugar
- 1/2 cup vegetable broth
- Fresh basil or cilantro for garnish

Instructions:

1. Heat vegetable oil in a large pan over medium heat. Add onion and bell pepper, and cook for 3-4 minutes until softened.
2. Add zucchini and snap peas, and cook for an additional 2 minutes.
3. Stir in coconut milk, green curry paste, soy sauce, brown sugar, and vegetable broth. Bring to a simmer and cook for 10 minutes, stirring occasionally.
4. Taste and adjust seasoning if necessary.

5. Serve the curry hot, garnished with fresh basil or cilantro.

Grilled Salmon with Avocado Salsa

Ingredients:

- 4 salmon fillets
- Olive oil for brushing
- Salt and pepper to taste
- 2 avocados, diced
- 1/2 red onion, diced
- 1 tomato, diced
- 1 jalapeño, seeded and minced
- 2 tbsp fresh cilantro, chopped
- 1 tbsp lime juice

Instructions:

1. Preheat the grill to medium-high heat. Brush the salmon fillets with olive oil and season with salt and pepper.
2. Grill the salmon for 4-5 minutes per side, or until cooked to your desired doneness.
3. While the salmon cooks, make the avocado salsa by combining diced avocados, red onion, tomato, jalapeño, cilantro, and lime juice in a bowl. Stir gently to combine.
4. Serve the grilled salmon with a generous spoonful of avocado salsa on top.

Baked Brie with Fig Jam

Ingredients:

- 1 wheel of Brie cheese (8 oz)
- 1/4 cup fig jam
- Fresh thyme or rosemary for garnish
- Crackers or baguette slices for serving

Instructions:

1. Preheat oven to 350°F (175°C).
2. Place the Brie cheese on a baking sheet lined with parchment paper.
3. Spread fig jam over the top of the Brie.
4. Bake for 10-12 minutes, until the Brie is soft and melted.
5. Garnish with fresh thyme or rosemary.
6. Serve with crackers or slices of baguette.

Prosciutto-Wrapped Asparagus

Ingredients:

- 12 asparagus spears, trimmed
- 6 slices prosciutto, halved lengthwise
- Olive oil for drizzling
- Salt and pepper to taste
- Fresh lemon wedges for serving

Instructions:

1. Preheat the oven to 400°F (200°C).
2. Wrap each asparagus spear with a slice of prosciutto.
3. Place the wrapped asparagus on a baking sheet and drizzle with olive oil. Season with salt and pepper.
4. Bake for 12-15 minutes, until the prosciutto is crispy and the asparagus is tender.
5. Serve with fresh lemon wedges.

Braised Lamb Shanks

Ingredients:

- 2 lamb shanks
- Salt and pepper to taste
- 2 tbsp olive oil
- 1 onion, chopped
- 2 carrots, chopped
- 3 cloves garlic, minced
- 1 cup red wine
- 2 cups beef broth
- 2 sprigs fresh rosemary
- 2 sprigs fresh thyme

Instructions:

1. Preheat oven to 325°F (165°C).
2. Season lamb shanks with salt and pepper.
3. Heat olive oil in a large ovenproof pot over medium-high heat. Brown the lamb shanks on all sides, about 8-10 minutes. Remove from the pot and set aside.
4. In the same pot, add onion, carrots, and garlic. Cook for 5 minutes until softened.
5. Pour in red wine and broth, scraping up any brown bits from the bottom of the pot. Return lamb shanks to the pot.

6. Add rosemary and thyme, then cover the pot and place it in the oven.

7. Braise for 2-3 hours, until the lamb is tender and easily falls off the bone.

8. Serve with the braising liquid.

Vegetable Paella

Ingredients:

- 1 tbsp olive oil
- 1 onion, chopped
- 1 red bell pepper, chopped
- 1 zucchini, chopped
- 1 cup frozen peas
- 1 cup Arborio rice
- 2 cups vegetable broth
- 1/4 tsp saffron threads
- 1 tsp smoked paprika
- Salt and pepper to taste
- Fresh parsley for garnish

Instructions:

1. Heat olive oil in a large pan over medium heat. Add onion, bell pepper, and zucchini, cooking for 5 minutes until softened.
2. Stir in Arborio rice and cook for 2-3 minutes, toasting the rice lightly.
3. In a small bowl, dissolve saffron in a little vegetable broth. Add this, along with the smoked paprika, to the pan.
4. Add the rest of the vegetable broth and bring to a simmer. Cover the pan and cook for 20-25 minutes, until the rice is tender and the liquid is absorbed.

5. Stir in frozen peas and cook for another 2 minutes.

6. Garnish with fresh parsley before serving.

Spicy Tuna Roll Sushi

Ingredients:

- 2 cups sushi rice, cooked and cooled
- 1 sheet nori (seaweed)
- 1/2 lb sushi-grade tuna, diced
- 1 tbsp soy sauce
- 1 tbsp sriracha sauce
- 1/2 tsp sesame oil
- 1/4 cucumber, julienned
- 1/4 avocado, sliced
- Soy sauce for dipping

Instructions:

1. In a bowl, mix diced tuna with soy sauce, sriracha sauce, and sesame oil. Set aside.
2. Place a sheet of nori on a bamboo sushi mat. Spread a thin layer of sushi rice over the nori, leaving a 1-inch border at the top.
3. Place a few pieces of tuna mixture, cucumber, and avocado along the center of the rice.
4. Roll the sushi tightly using the bamboo mat, sealing the edge with a little water.
5. Slice the roll into 6-8 pieces and serve with soy sauce for dipping.